Four Faces in Rock

by Stacey Zable

Table of Contents

What Are the Four Faces in Rock? 2
How Big Is Mount Rushmore? 8
How Was Mount Rushmore Made? 10
What Is Mount Rushmore Like Today? 14
Glossary and Index 16

What Are the Four Faces in Rock?

What has eight eyes, four noses, four mouths and chins, and no ears?

Mount Rushmore!

Mount Rushmore is a national memorial. It was built to honor the birth and growth of the United States of America.

Mount Rushmore is a mountain. It is also a national **memorial**. The faces of four American presidents are carved into the mountain.

Mount Rushmore is one of the largest works of art in the world. It is so big that you can see it from 60 **miles** away!

60 miles

Can you name the faces you see on Mount Rushmore?

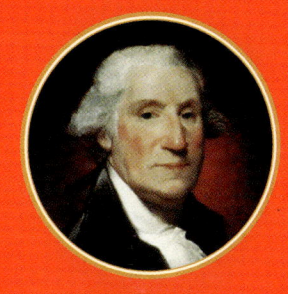

George Washington

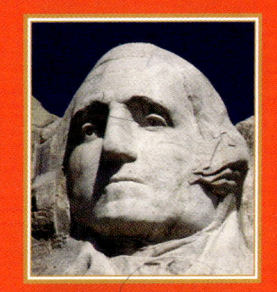

Abraham Lincoln

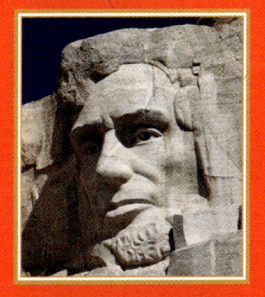

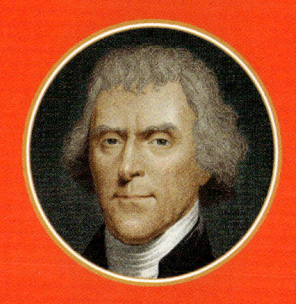

Thomas Jefferson

Theodore Roosevelt

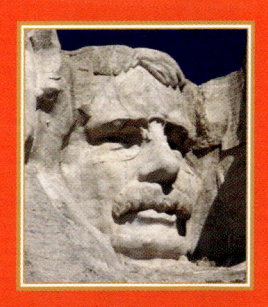

Mount Rushmore is in the Black Hills of South Dakota. These mountains span more than one million **acres** of land in South Dakota and Wyoming.

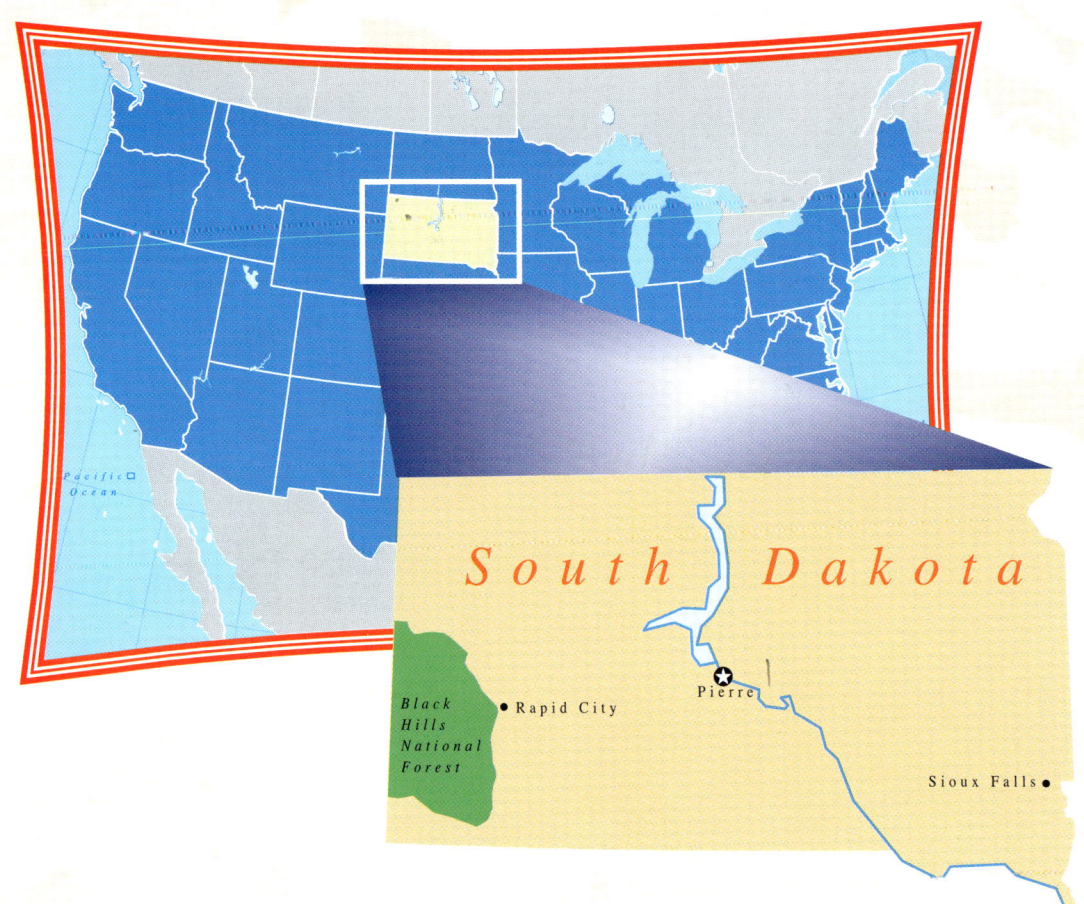

Mount Rushmore covers more than one thousand acres of the Black Hills. It is about 25 miles from Rapid City, South Dakota.

South Dakota

Mt. Rushmore
National Memorial
1,000 acres

25 miles ● Rapid City

**Black Hills
National Forest**
Over 1 million acres

WYOMING

7

How Big Is Mount Rushmore?

Mount Rushmore stands more than five thousand feet tall. Each face on the mountain is about 60 feet (720 inches) tall. That is eighty times bigger than most people's faces.

If the whole bodies of each president were carved, they would stand about 465 feet tall!

face: 60 feet tall

mouth: 18 feet wide

moustache: 20 feet wide

eye: 11 feet wide

465 feet

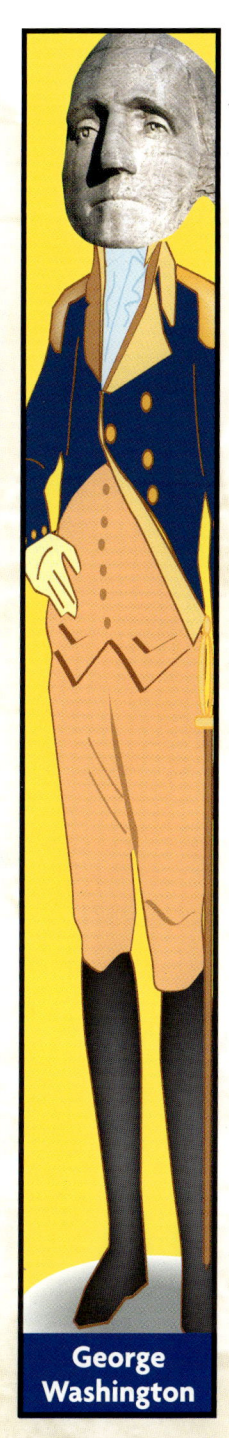

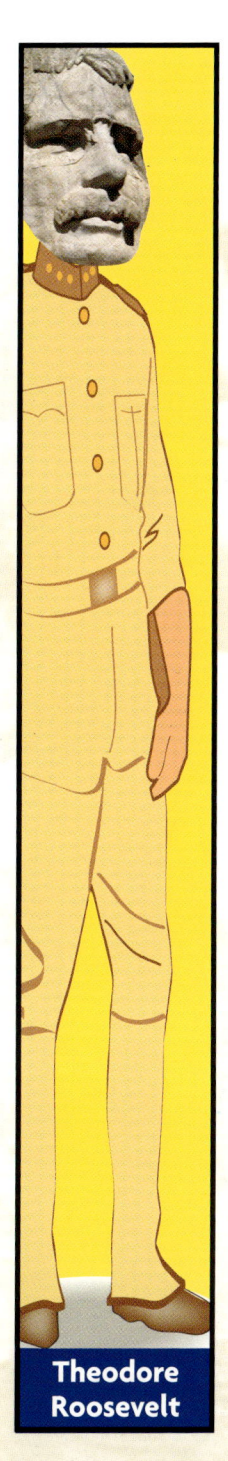

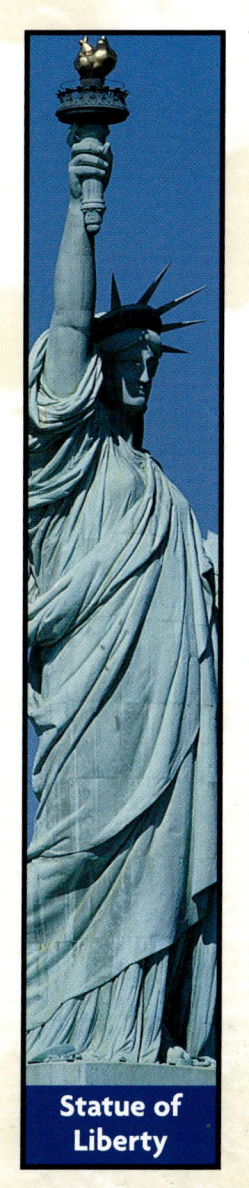

305 feet

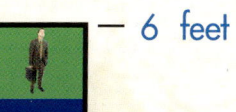

6 feet

George Washington

Theodore Roosevelt

Statue of Liberty

person

Figures not to scale

9

How Was Mount Rushmore Made?

A man named Gutzon Borglum made the four faces.

First, Borglum made small **models** of the faces using old paintings and photographs of the presidents.

A measurement of one inch on the model equaled one foot on the mountain.

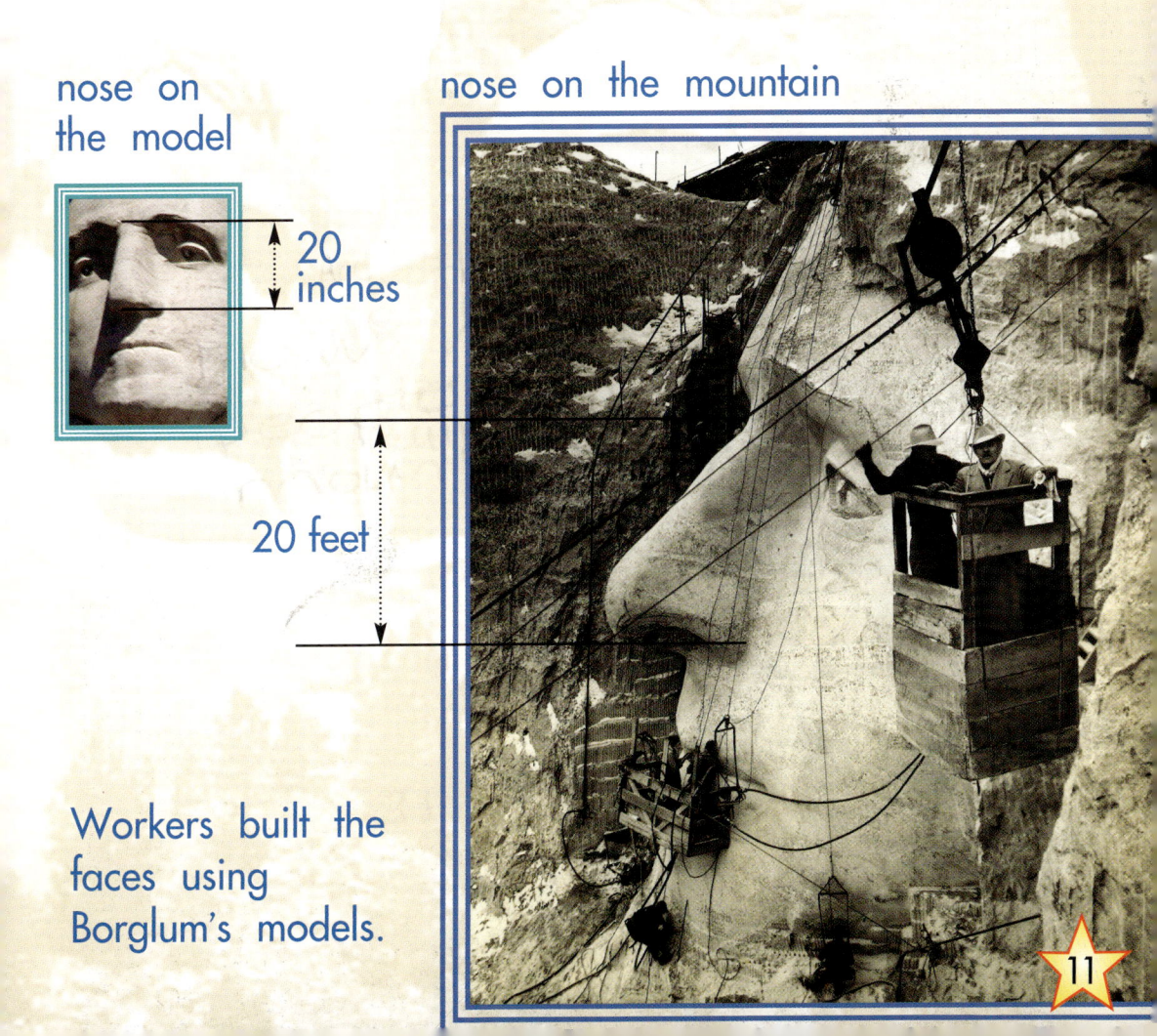

nose on the model

nose on the mountain

20 inches

20 feet

Workers built the faces using Borglum's models.

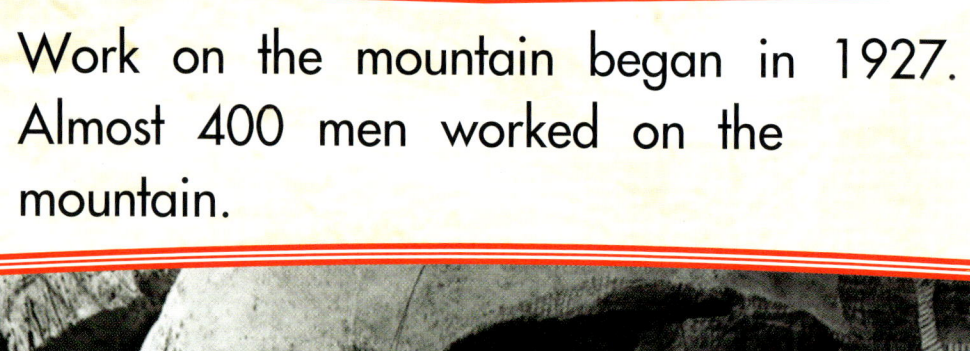

Work on the mountain began in 1927. Almost 400 men worked on the mountain.

To do the work, **cables** less than one inch wide were fastened to the mountain. Workers hung from the ends of the cables in small saddles. From the saddles, they used dynamite and hand tools to cut the faces into the rock.

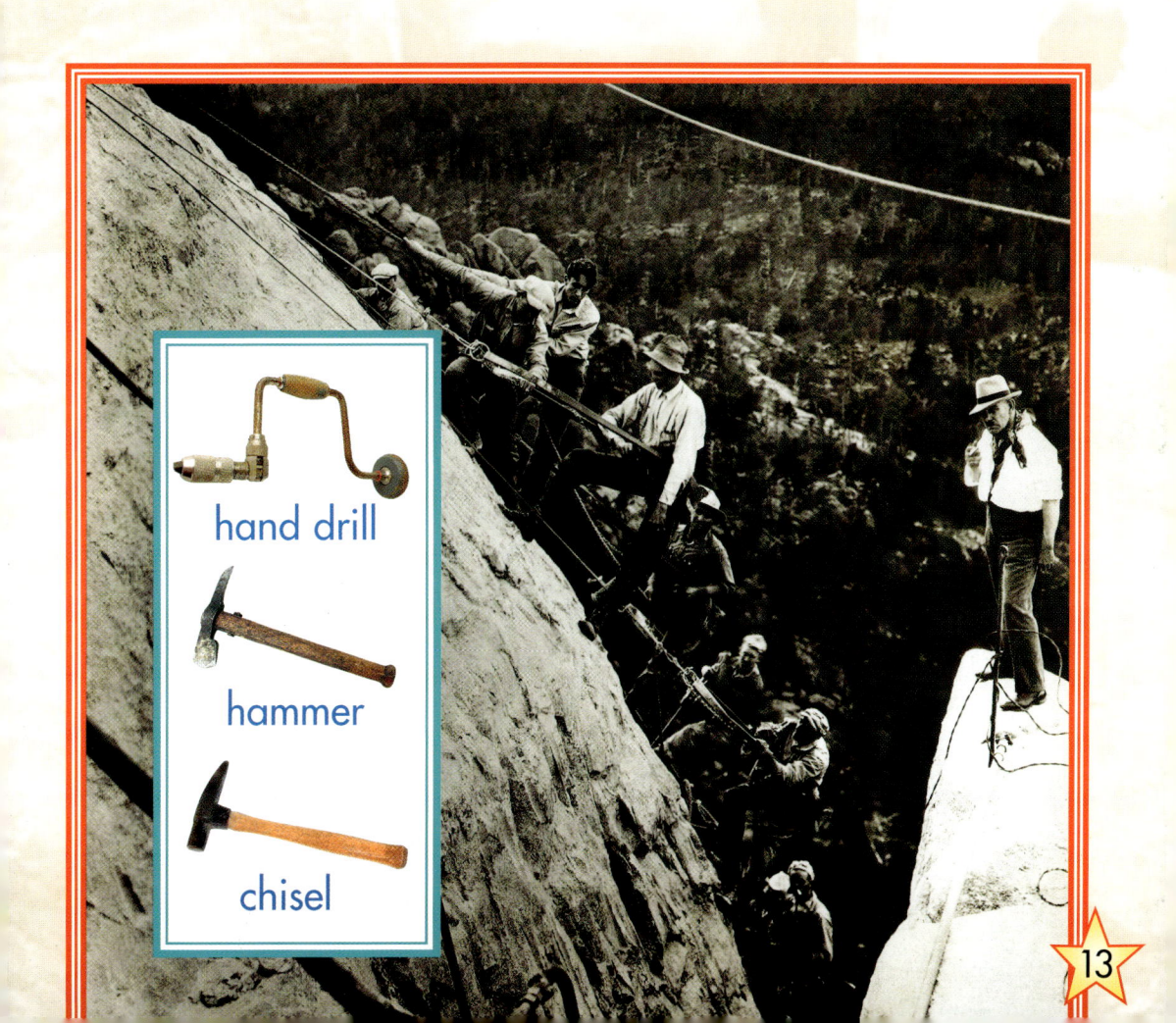

hand drill

hammer

chisel

What Is Mount Rushmore Like Today?

The four faces on Mount Rushmore greet more than two million visitors each year.

It took fourteen years and one million dollars to finish carving the faces in the mountain. Today, we think of Mount Rushmore as **priceless**.

Mount Rushmore National Memorial is a popular place to visit.

Glossary

acre (AY-kur): a unit for measuring land; 43,560 square feet

cable (CAY-bul): a thick, strong rope made of twisted fiber or wire

memorial (meh-MOR-ee-ul): something built or done to remember a person, group of people, or event

mile (MY-uhl): a unit for measuring distance; 5,280 feet

model (MAH-dul): a small copy of something

priceless (PRYS-less): having great worth

Index

Black Hills, 6–7

Borglum, Gutzon, 10–11

Jefferson, Thomas, 5

Lincoln, Abraham, 5

Roosevelt, Theodore, 5, 9

South Dakota, 6–7

Washington, George, 5, 9

Wyoming, 6–7